folding
with greetings

**Maruscha Gaasenbeek
and Tine Beauveser**

FORTE PUBLISHERS

Contents

Eight printing February 2004
ISBN 90 5877 270 5

This is a publication from
Forte Publishers BV
P.O. Box 1394
3500 BJ Utrecht
The Netherlands

For more information about the creative books available from Forte Uitgevers:
www.hobby-party.com

Publisher: Marianne Perlot
Editor: Hanny Vlaar
Photography and digital image editing:
Fotografie Gerhard Witteveen, Apeldoorn, the Netherlands
Cover : Studio Herman Bade BV, Baarn, the Netherlands
Inner design: Elgraphic+DTQP bv, Schiedam, the Netherlands
Translation: TextCase, Groningen, the Netherlands

Preface

A new springtime, a new season and new IRIS folding patterns in this book. The cards in this book **IRIS Folding® with Greetings** are filled with the insides of envelopes which have been cut into strips. The possibilities offered by this free material are almost endless. Nowadays, most people have a box next to their waste paper bin to save old envelopes for their friend, sister, neighbour, niece in Canada or even themselves. The greater the number of different envelopes you have, the better the IRIS folding cards. Thanks to your enthusiastic reactions to our text sheets, we have now made special greetings sheets to use with the patterns in this book. These are real *greetings* cards, because the greeting is included in the pattern of many of the cards given in this book. The colourful IRIS folding text stickers also go perfectly with every card. Do you also have a large number of blue envelopes? We have 194 in our total collection of 512. That is why we have used a lot of blue this time. A number of punches have been used in a surprising way and it is fun to try them out. The contrasting sheets of envelope paper have been used in different ways. So, get started as quickly as possible because, as you know, an IRIS folding card makes two people happy: the person who receives the card and the person who has made it.

Have fun!

Maruscha Gaasenbeek

Techniques

The starting point for IRIS folding is the pattern. Cut the outer shape of the pattern out of the card and then fill the hole from the outside to the inside with folded strips of used envelopes. You work at the back of the card, so you work, in fact, on a mirror image. And when you have finished, you stick it onto another card. For an oval pattern, select four different envelopes where the patterns and colours combine and contrast nicely with each other. Cut all the envelopes into strips in the same way, for example, from left to right. Depending on the pattern, you will need between four and eight strips. The width of the strips also depends on the pattern and is stated for each card. You need to first fold one border of the strips over and sort them into each different type of envelope. Next, you cover each section in turn by following the numbers (1, 2, 3, 4, 5, etc.), so that you rotate the pattern. Lay the strips with the fold facing towards the middle of the pattern and then stick them to the left and right-hand sides of the card using adhesive tape. Finally, use an attractive piece of deco tape or holographic paper to cover the hole in the middle. Avoid colour differences by using one envelope for the same design.

The oval
(see Step-by-step, no. 4)
The most important thing is to start with the basic oval, because from this, you will learn the unique folding and sticking technique needed for all the patterns. You will notice that you quickly get used to the technique of IRIS folding.

Preparation
1. Use the oval Coluzzle template, the special cutting mat and the pivoting knife to cut the oval (8 x 6 cm) out of the blue card (13.8 x 9.5 cm).
2. Stick a copy of the basic oval given in this book (pattern 1) on an ordinary cutting mat using adhesive tape.
3. Turn the card over and place it on the oval pattern (you should be looking at the back of the card) with the hole exactly on the pattern and only stick the left-hand side of the card to your cutting mat using masking tape.
4. Select three envelopes with different blue patterns and take the blue greetings sheet.
5. Cut 2 cm wide strips from the envelopes and approximately 1.6 cm wide strips from the greetings sheet. Make groups of colour A, colour B, colour C and colour D.

1. The inside of one hundred and ninety four different blue envelopes!

2. Cut the oval out of the back of a single card. Cut the envelopes and greetings sheets into strips and fold the edge over.

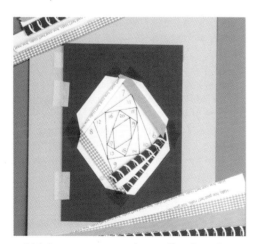

3. Stick the pattern to your cutting mat. Place the card on top and stick down the left-hand side. Place the strips exactly against the line and stick down the left and right-hand sides using adhesive tape.

4. Fold the card open from time to time to see whether the patterns continue nicely.

6. For each strip, fold a border along the entire length with the nice side facing outwards.

IRIS folding

7. Take a folded strip of colour A and place it over section 1, exactly against the line of the pattern with the folded side facing towards the middle. Allow 0.5 cm to stick out on the left and right-hand sides and cut the rest off. By doing so, the strip will also slightly stick over the edge of the pattern at the bottom, so that section 1 is totally covered.

8. Stick the strip to the card on the left and right-hand sides using a small piece of adhesive tape, but remain 0.5 cm from the edge of the card.

9. Take a strip of colour B and place it on section 2 of the pattern. Also tape this to the card on the left and right-hand sides.

10. Take a strip of colour C. Place this on section 3 and stick it into place.

11. Take a strip of colour D. Place this on section 4 and stick it into place.

12. Start again with colour A on section 5, colour B on section 6, colour C on section 7 and colour D on section 8.
    The strips on sections 1, 5, 9, 13 and 17 of this pattern are all of colour A. The strips on sections 2, 6, 10, 14 and 18 are all of colour B. The strips on sections 3, 7, 11, 15, and 19 are all of colour C. The strips on sections 4, 8, 12, 16, and 20 are all of colour D.

Finishing

After section 20, carefully remove the card. Stick a piece of holographic paper in the middle on the back of the card. You can use punches, corner scissors and bits of envelope paper to add an extra finishing touch to the card. The corners of this card have been punched out using the *Spear* corner punch. Stick small pieces of double-sided adhesive tape along the edges, remove the protective layer and fix your work to a double card. Do not use glue, because all the paper strips place pressure on the card.

Making greetings strips

Cut the A4 greetings sheet into four and take the piece which suits the envelopes you have picked the best. Leave the first line of greetings and cut the second line horizontally through the middle. Leave the third line and cut the fourth line through the middle. This will produce approximately 1.6 cm wide strips which you can use instead of a group of envelope strips. When working at the top of a pattern, fold the coloured border under the text. To make a straight fold, score a line on the back of the strip by running a needle along a ruler.

Cutting tips

1. Copy the bow (page 24) onto the back of a piece of paper. Place a piece of paper of another colour back to front behind it. Staple them together and cut them out to make two different bows.
2. To cover large areas, place a piece of paper over the area so that more than the area is covered and cut accurately only the side of the pattern.
3. For double shapes, copy the drawing onto one side of the paper. Fold it double along the dotted line. Staple it together and cut it out.

Materials

To make the cards:
- ❑ Card: Canson Mi-Teintes (C), Artoz (A), Papicolor (P) and Romak (R)
- ❑ Sheets of envelope paper
- ❑ IRIS folding greetings sheets
- ❑ IRIS folding text stickers
- ❑ Cutting knife
- ❑ Cutting mat
- ❑ Ruler with a metal cutting edge (Securit)
- ❑ Adhesive tape
- ❑ Double-sided adhesive tape
- ❑ Masking tape
- ❑ Various punches (TomTas, Make Me!, Media)
- ❑ Multi-corner punch (Reuser)

- ❑ 3-in-1 corner punches (Fiskars)
- ❑ Punch (Fiskars)
- ❑ Border ornament punches (Fiskars)
- ❑ Punch with exchangeable shapes (TomTas)
- ❑ Scissors and silhouette scissors
- ❑ Corner and figure scissors (Fiskars)
- ❑ Photo glue
- ❑ Oval Coluzzle template, cutting mat and pivoting knife
- ❑ Light box

IRIS folding
- ❑ Strips of used envelopes
- ❑ IRIS folding greetings sheets

The middle of the card
- ❑ Deco tape
- ❑ Holographic paper

The patterns:
Full-size examples of all the patterns are given in this book. Draw around the circumference using a light box. The shapes are usually easy to cut out of the card. Specially punched cards are available for the crocus, the birth spoon, the watering can, the fish and the 2CV.

Ovals

Delightful colours caught in a classic oval with special corners.

All the cards are made according to the instructions given for the basic oval (8 x 6 cm) (see Techniques).

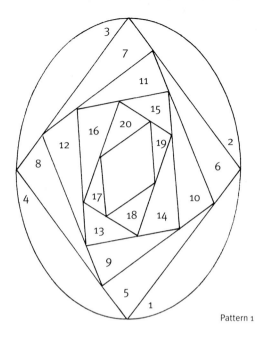

Pattern 1

Card 1

Card: blue P31 (14.8 x 21 cm) and pearl grey C120 (13.8 x 9.5 cm) • Pattern 1 • 2 cm wide strips from 4 different blue envelopes • Blue paper (10 x 8 cm) • Silver holographic paper • Oval Coluzzle template • Mini scallop figure scissors, Mosaic punch (Art)

Punch out the corners of the small card using the mosaic punch. Cut out the oval and fill it with the strips. Next, cut an oval (8 x 6 cm) out of the sheet of envelope paper, fold the sheet double twice and staple it together. Draw a line 0.6 cm from the side as shown in the diagram (see page 13) and use the teeth of the figure scissors to cut along the line. Stick the frame on the IRIS folding oval.

Card 2

Card: petrol (14.8 x 21 cm) and white (13.8 x 9.5 cm) • Pattern 1 • 2 cm wide strips from 4 blue/green envelopes • Silver deco tape • Mosaic punch (Flower)

Card 3

Card: soft blue C102 (14.8 x 21 cm) and sea green (13.5 x 9.4 cm) • Pattern 1 • 2 cm wide strips from 3 different green/blue envelopes • 1.6 cm wide strips from the blue greetings sheet • Text sticker • Silver holographic paper • Oval Coluzzle template • 3-in-1 corner punch (Lace)

Stick the text sticker on envelope paper and cut it out with a 1 mm border.

Card 4

Card: dark blue (14.8 x 21 cm) and lilac C104 (13.8 x 9.5 cm) • Pattern 1 • 2 cm wide strips from 3 different blue and grey envelopes • 1.6 cm wide strips from the blue greetings sheet • Silver holographic paper • Oval Coluzzle template • Mosaic punch (Circle)
Punch out the corners of the lilac card using a quarter of the mosaic punch pattern. After finishing the IRIS folding, make four blue streamers and stick them to the oval.

Card 5

Card: light blue C102 (14.8 x 21 cm) and indigo blue C140 (13.7 x 9.2 cm) • Pattern 1 • 2 cm wide strips from 4 different sea green envelopes • Sheet of turquoise paper (14.2 x 9.7 cm) • Silver holographic paper • Oval Coluzzle template • Mosaic punch (Spear)

Card 6

Card: sea green (14.8 x 21 cm) and off-white C335 (13.8 x 9.5 cm) • Pattern 1 • 2 cm wide strips from 4 different blue/green envelopes • Silver holographic paper • Oval Coluzzle template • Mosaic punch (Spear)

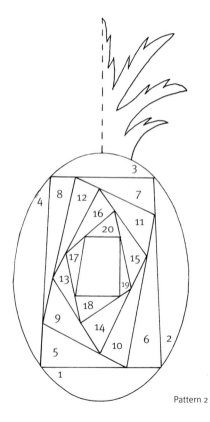

Pattern 2

Playing with ovals

An exotic, fruity card and a card

with a twist.

The pineapple card is made according to the instructions given for card 1. The large oval is made according to the instructions given for card 5.

Card 1

Card: mango A575 (14.8 x 21 cm) and Primavera embossed champagne (13.8 x 9.5 cm) • Pattern 2 • 2 cm wide strips from 4 different orange/brown envelopes • Green and orange paper (5 x 5 cm) for the leaf • Text sticker • Gold holographic paper • Oval Coluzzle template • Corner scissors (Nostalgia) Punch out the corners of the small card and cut out the oval (6.6 x 4.8 cm). Stick the two bunches of leaves on top of each other so that the bottom bunch is slightly visible.

Card 2

Card: soft yellow (14.8 x 21 cm and 14.3 x 8.5 cm) • Sheet of green paper (14.3 x 9.2 cm) • Pattern 2 • 2 cm wide strips from 4 different green and yellow envelopes • Liver coloured paper for the leaf (5 x 5 cm) • Text sticker • Gold deco tape • Oval Coluzzle template

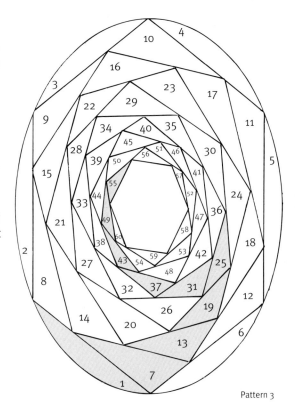

Pattern 3

Card 3

Card: carnation white P03 (14.8 x 21 cm) and salmon beige C384 (13.8 x 8.5 cm) • Sheet of green paper (14.2 x 9.8 cm) • Pattern 2 • 2 cm wide strips from 4 different beige/yellow envelopes • Beige paper for the leaf (5 x 5 cm) • Gold holographic paper • Oval Coluzzle template • Regal corner scissors • Border figure punch (Lace)

Card 4

Card: apple green C475 (14.8 x 21 cm), butter yellow C400 (14 x 9.8 cm) and Firenze embossed beige (13.5 x 8.8 cm). Pattern 2 • 2 cm wide strips from 4 different green and orange envelopes • Orange and green paper for the leaf (5 x 5 cm) • Gold deco tape • Oval Coluzzle template

Card 5

Card: salmon oval punch card R64 (14.8 x 21 cm) and brown covering card (14.5 x 10 cm) • Pattern 3 • 2 cm wide strips from 6 different beige/brown envelopes • Silver holographic paper

Open the double card and place the good side on the pattern. The pattern changes after sections 25 to 30. Just follow the numbers and

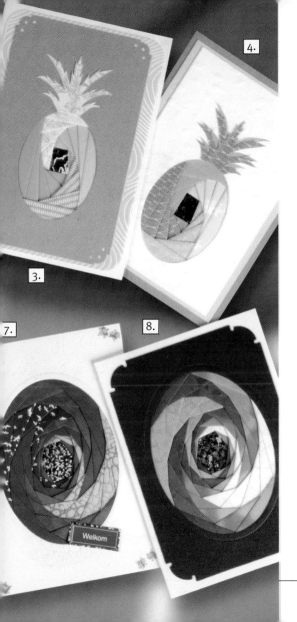

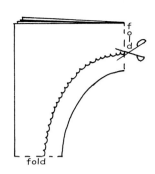

0.25 frame

keep the same colour order. To help you, the sections for colour A have been shaded.

Card 6
Card: aubergine oval punch card R26 (14.8 x 21 cm) and red covering card (14.5 x 10 cm) • Pattern 3 • 2 cm wide strips from 6 different pink/orange/red envelopes • Silver holographic paper

Card 7
Card: salmon oval punch card R64 (14.8 x 21 cm) and pink covering card (14.5 x 10 cm) • Pattern 3 • 6 groups of 2 cm wide strips from 4 different blue/red envelopes • Text sticker • Silver holographic paper • Mini-punch (Leaf)

Card 8
Card: salmon R64 (14.8 x 21 cm) and red R23 oval punch card (13.8 x 9.7 cm) ˌ Pattern 3 • 6 groups of 2 cm wide strips from 4 different orange/blue/grey envelopes • Silver holographic paper • Corner punch (Lily)

Birth spoon

We are glad to announce

the birth of ...

All the cards are made according to the instructions given for card 1 (also see cutting tip 1).

Card 1

Card: maize C470 (21 x 10.3 cm) and lemon yellow C101 (19 x 8.6 cm) • Sheet of yellow paper (19.6 x 9.3 cm) • Pattern 4 • 5 groups of 2 cm wide strips from 4 different yellow envelopes • Gold deco tape • 20 cm of yellow ribbon • 3-in-1 corner punch (Lace) • Bear punch • Orange pencil • Hole punch

Punch out the top corners of the small card and cut the spoon out of the back. Cover the handle and cut the bottom to the same shape as the pattern. After finishing the IRIS folding, stick the bears on the card and mark the handle with the coloured pencil. Stick a ribbon on the card so that it can be hung up.

Card 2

Card: ice blue P42 (21 x 10.3 cm), IRIS blue P31 (20 x 9.5 cm) and white (19 x 9 cm) • Pattern 4 • 4 groups of 2 cm wide strips from 3 different blue envelopes • 1.6 cm wide strips from the

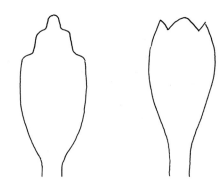

blue greetings sheet • Silver holographic paper • 20 cm of blue ribbon

Card 3

Card: pink C352 (21 x 10.3 cm) and white (18.6 x 10.5 cm), Pattern 4 • 2 cm wide strips from 4 different pink envelopes • 1.6 cm wide strips from the red greetings sheet • Silver holographic paper • Border ornament punch (Heart) • Punch (Duck) • 20 cm of ribbon

Punch out the edges of the white card so that the card is 9.4 cm wide.

Card 4

Card: azure P04 (21 x 10.5 cm), turquoise P32 (20.2 x 9.8 cm) and white (19.8 x 9.3 cm) • Pattern 4 • 5 groups of 4 different sea green envelopes • Silver holographic paper • Text sticker • Punch (Bear) • Corner punch (Heart)

Card 5

Card: cerise P33 (21 x 10 cm) and white (19.7 x 8.5 cm) • Pattern 4 • 2 cm wide strips from 4 different pink envelopes • 1.6 cm wide strips from the red greetings sheet • Pink paper (8 x 6.5 cm) for the bow and the letters • Silver deco tape • Punch (Girl)

Card 6

Card: birch green A305 (21 x 10 cm) and white (19 x 6.5 cm) • Sheet of green paper (19.7 x 9.5 cm) • Pattern 4 • 2 cm wide strips from 5 different green envelopes • Gold holographic paper • Text sticker • Border ornament punch (Heart) • Punch (Rabbit)
Punch out hearts along the sides of the sheet of green paper 0.5 cm from the top and bottom.

Card 7

Card: royal blue A427 (21 x 10 cm) and white (19 x 8 cm) • Pattern 4 • 2 cm wide strips from 5 different blue envelopes • 2 cm wide strip from the blue greetings sheet for the handle ˌ Silver deco tape • Multi-corner punch • Mini-punch (Hand)

Card 8

Card: honey yellow A243 (21 x 10 cm and for the handle 10 x 2 cm) and beige scented card (19.3 x 8.3 cm) • Sheet of orange paper (19.8 x 8.7 cm) • Pattern 4 • 2 cm wide strips from 5 different yellow/orange envelopes • Orange paper (7 x 6.5 cm) for the bow • Gold holographic paper • Exchangeable figure punch (Crown) • Orange pencil • Regal corner punch

Pattern 4

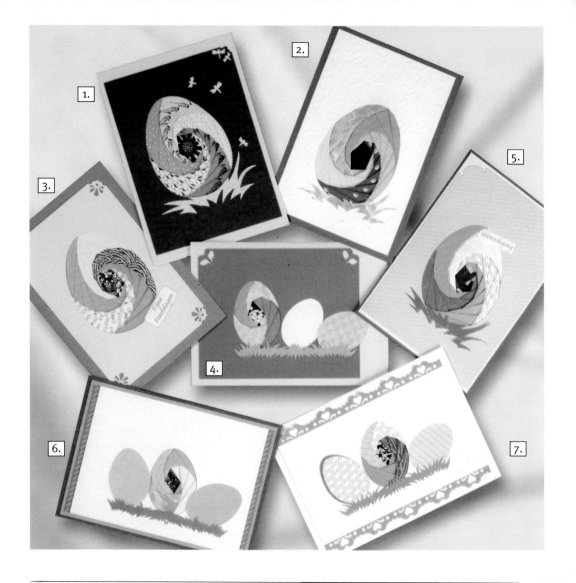

1.

2.

3.

4.

5.

6.

7.

Big eggs and little eggs

One egg is no egg, two eggs is half

an egg, three eggs is an extravagance.

The big egg is made according to the description given for card 1 and the small eggs according to the description given for card 4.

Pattern 5

Card 1
Card: sea green P17 (14.8 x 21 cm) and Antica grey blue P165 (14.8 x 10.5 cm) • Pattern 5 • 2 cm wide strips from 5 different grey envelopes • Grey/green paper for the grass (4 x 9 cm) • Silver deco tape • 3-in-1 corner punch (Bugs) Punch out the top right-hand corner of the small card and cut the egg out of the back. Copy the grass using the light box.

Card 2
Card: petrol (14.8 x 21 cm) and Primavera embossed champagne (14.1 x 9.5 cm) • Pattern 5 • 2 cm wide strips from 5 different sea green and yellow envelopes • Sea green paper for the grass (4 x 9 cm) • Gold deco tape

Card 3
Card: smoke blue C490 (14.8 x 21 cm) and sea green P17 (13.3 x 9 cm) • Pattern 5 • 2 cm wide strips from 5 different light green and grey envelopes • Silver deco tape • Text sticker • Multi-corner punch

Card 4
Card: shell white C112 (14.8 x 21 cm) and rust brown C504 (12 x 9.5 cm) • Pattern 6 • 2 cm wide strips from 4 different beige envelopes • 2

Half of the grass border

pieces of beige paper for the decorative eggs (5 x 4 cm) • Pale green paper for the grass (2 x 10 cm) • Gold holographic paper • 3-in-1 corner punch (Leaves)

Punch out the top corners of the small card and cut the small egg out of the back. Decorate the card with extra eggs and the open folded grass.

Card 5

Card: petrol (14.8 x 21 cm), ivory white C110 (14.4 x 10 cm) and peach pink (14 x 9.7 cm) • Pattern 5 • 5 groups of 2 cm wide strips from 4 different beige, brown and sea green envelopes • Brown paper for the grass (4 x 9 cm) • Silver holographic paper • Text sticker • Corner punch (Tulip)

Card 6

Card: brown (14.8 x 21 cm), mango A575 (14.2 x 10 cm) and white C335 (12.9 x 9.5 cm) • Pattern 6 • 2 cm wide strips from 4 different yellow/greyish blue envelopes • 2 cm wide strips of brown paper for the border ornament and the grass • Yellow and beige paper for the decorative eggs (5 x 4 cm) • Gold deco tape • Border ornament punch (Rope)

Card 7

Card: white C335 (14.8 x 21 cm and 13.7 x 8 cm) • Brown sheet of envelope paper (13.7 x 11 cm) • Pattern 6 • 2 cm wide strips from 4 different brown envelopes • 3 pieces of brown paper for the decorative eggs (5 x 4 cm) • Green paper for the grass (2 x 10 cm) • Copper deco tape • Border ornament punch (Heart)

Punch out the top and bottom of the sheet of envelope paper so that it measures 13.7 x 9.8 cm.

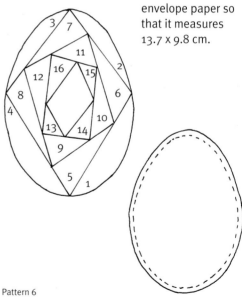

Pattern 6

2CV

A card to send to speedy drivers or somebody who has just past their driving test.

All the cards are made according to the instructions given for card 1 (also see cutting tip 2). Use a circle template for the wheels.

Card 1

Card: white (14.8 x 21 cm and 13.8 x 9 cm) • Sheet of red paper (14.8 x 9.7 cm) • Pattern 7 • 2 cm wide strips from 3 different red envelopes • 1.6 cm wide strips from the red greetings sheet • Orange paper for A (2.5 x 4.5 cm) • Red paper for B and C (8 x 6 cm) • Dark brown paper for the wheels (2.5 x 5 cm) • Copper deco tape • 2-in-1 border punch (Balloon)

Cut the 2CV without the wheels out of the back of the small card according to the pattern. Use the light box to copy part A onto orange paper and parts B and C onto red paper. Note: follow the line of the large section exactly and draw the rest so that it is 0.5 cm bigger. Cut everything out, then cover section A, section B and section C and stick them into place using adhesive tape. After finishing the IRIS folding,

draw the wheels (2.1 cm) on the brown paper and cut them out. Punch out the balloon and cut out the *birds*.

Card 2

Card: white (14.8 x 21 cm and 13.7 x 8.5 cm) • Sheet of blue paper (8 x 13.7 cm) and strips from the blue greetings sheet (2 x 0.8 cm) • Pattern 7 • 2 cm wide strips from 4 different blue envelopes • Blue paper for A and C (8 x 5 cm) and light blue paper for B (3 x 4.5 cm) • Dark blue paper for the wheels (2.5 x 5 cm) • Silver holographic paper

After finishing the IRIS folding, stick the strips from the greetings sheet at the top and bottom of the small card and fill it up with the sheet of blue paper.

Card 3

Card: petrol (14.8 x 21 cm) and white C335 (13.8 x 9.5 cm) • Sheet of yellow/green paper (14.1 x 9.8 cm) • Pattern 7 • 2 cm wide strips from 4 different blue/green envelopes • Green paper for A (2.5 x 4.5 cm) and petrol paper for B and C (8 x 6 cm) • Dark green paper for the wheels (2.5 x 5 cm) • Silver holographic paper • Text sticker • Regal corner scissors

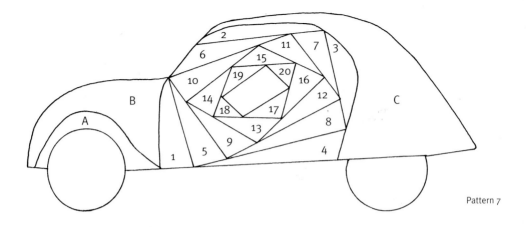

Pattern 7

Card 4

Card: mid-grey (14.8 x 21 cm), red (14.1 x 9.8 cm) and white C335 (13.9 x 9.6 cm) • Sheet of light grey paper (14.5 x 10.2 cm) • Pattern 7 • 2 cm wide strips from 4 different grey envelopes • Light grey paper for A (2.5 x 4.5 cm) and dark grey paper for B and C (8 x 6 cm) • Strip from the red greetings sheet • Silver holographic paper • Mosaic punch (Spear)
Use a part of the punch for the top corners of the small card.

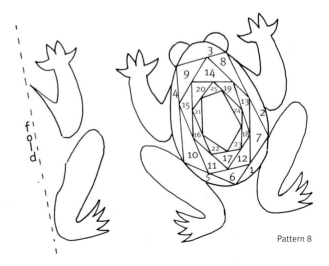

Pattern 8

Frogs and fishes

Jump like a frog and swim like a fish.

The frogs are made according to the instructions given for the card on the cover. The fish are made according to the instructions given for card 4.

Card on the cover
Card: blue (9 x 18 cm) and white (8 x 8 cm) • Pattern 8 • 1.5 cm wide strips from 5 different blue/brown envelopes • Dark blue paper for the feet (7 x 5 cm) • Gold deco tape • Regal corner scissors • 3-in-1 corner punch (Bugs)
Punch out the top left-hand corner and cut the body of the frog out of the back of the white card. Copy the feet and the eyes using the light box (see the cutting tips and the diagram).

Card 1
Card: lilac C104 (14.8 x 21 cm) and grey/green (13.8 x 9.5 cm) • Pattern 8 • 1.5 cm wide strips from 5 different green envelopes • Green paper for the feet (7 x 5 cm) • Silver holographic paper • Punch (Frog)

Card 2
Card: sepia C133 (14.8 x 21 cm) and beige C407 (13.8 x 9.8 cm) • Pattern 8 • 1.5 cm wide strips

from 5 different brown envelopes • Two pieces of beige and brown paper for the feet (7 x 5 cm) • Gold holographic paper • 3-in-1 corner punch (Bugs)

Card 3
Card: white (14.8 x 21 cm and 14 x 9.5 cm) • Sheet of green paper (14.2 x 9.8 cm) • Pattern 8 • 1.5 cm wide strips from 5 different green envelopes • Two pieces of green paper for the feet (7 x 5 cm) • Silver holographic paper

Card 4
Card: lilac C104 (14.8 x 21 cm and 13.8 x 9.4 cm) • Sheet of light blue paper (14 x 9.8 cm) • Pattern 9 • 2 cm wide strips from 4 different blue envelopes • Blue paper for A and B (3 x 6 cm) • Silver holographic paper • Punch (Sea horse)
Cut the fish out of the back of the small card. Cover the head, the tail and the fins (see cutting tip 2). Cut the inside to exactly the same size as the pattern. Fill the body with the strips of envelope paper.

Card 5
Card: petrol (10.5 x 29.7 cm) and lilac C104 (9 x 13.8 cm) • Pattern 9 • 2 cm wide strips from 4

different turquoise envelopes • Sea green
paper (3 x 3 cm) and turquoise paper (3 x 3 cm)
for A and B • Silver holographic paper
Decorate the bottom of the card with a strip of
holographic paper which has been cut into the
shape of waves.

Card 6

*Card: white R21 (14.8 x 21 cm) and light blue
(13.8 x 10 cm) • Pattern 9 • 2 cm wide strips
from 3 different blue/green envelopes • Green
paper for A and B (3 x 6 cm) • 1.6 cm wide
strips from the blue greetings sheet • Silver
holographic paper • Border ornament punch
(Spring) • Multi-corner punch • Punch
(Dolphin)*

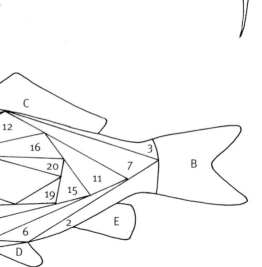

Pattern 9

Suitcases

"I'm going on holiday and

I'm taking ..."

The suitcases are made according
to the instructions given for card 1.

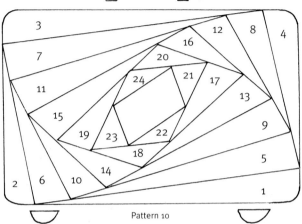

Pattern 10

Card 1
Card: violet P20 (13 x 26 cm) and dark
blue A417 (12 x 12 cm) • Sheet of blue
paper (12.4 x 12.4 cm) • Pattern 10 • 2
cm wide strips from 3 different blue
envelopes • 1.6 cm wide strips from the
blue greetings sheet • Silver holographic
paper • Text sticker • Multi-corner punch
Punch out the corners of the small card and cut
the suitcase out of the back. After finishing the
IRIS folding, stick the label, handle and wheels
on the card.

Card 2
Card: red P43 (14.8 x 21 cm), lime green (14.3 x
10 cm) and lily white C110 (13.8 x 9.5 cm) •
Pattern 10 • 2 cm wide strips from 4 different red
and green envelopes • Silver holographic paper
• Text sticker • Corner scissors (Nostalgia)
Cut the corners off of the white card using the
corner scissors.

Card 3
Card: royal blue A427 (13 x 26 cm) and white
(12 x 12 cm) • Pattern 10 • 2 cm wide strips
from 4 different blue envelopes • Silver
holographic paper • Text sticker • Corner
ornament punch (Spear)

Card 4
Card: fiesta red P12 (14.8 x 21 cm) and white
C335 (13.5 x 9.4 cm) • Pattern 10 • 2 cm wide
strips from 3 different grey and red envelopes •
1.6 cm wide strips from the red greetings sheet
• Silver holographic paper • 3-in-1 corner
punch (Heritage)

Card 5

Card: dark blue A417 (13 x 26 cm) and white (9.5 x 12 cm) • Sheet of blue/green paper (12.5 x 12.2 cm) • Pattern 10 • 2 cm wide strips from 4 different blue envelopes • Blue/green holographic paper • Text sticker • Mosaic punch (Circle)
Decorate the top and bottom of the blue/green paper with half of the pattern from the mosaic punch. Cut off the excess pieces.

Card 6

Card: indigo blue C140 (14.8 x 21 cm) and lemon yellow C101 (13.8 x 9.5 cm) • Pattern 10 • 2 cm wide strips from 3 different yellow/blue envelopes • 1.6 cm wide strips from the blue greetings sheet • Silver holographic paper • Text sticker • 3-in-1 corner punch (Lace)

Card 7

Card: white (13 x 26 cm) and lavender blue C150 (9.9 x 12 cm) • Beige paper (13.2 x 12.5 cm) • Pattern 10 • 2 cm wide strips from 4 different beige envelopes • Silver holographic paper • Border ornament punch (Spring)
Decorate the top and bottom of the beige paper using the border ornament punch so that the paper is 12 cm high.

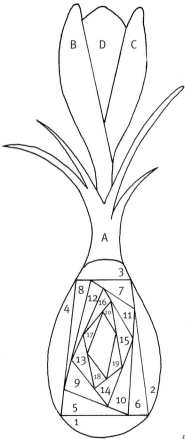

Pattern 11

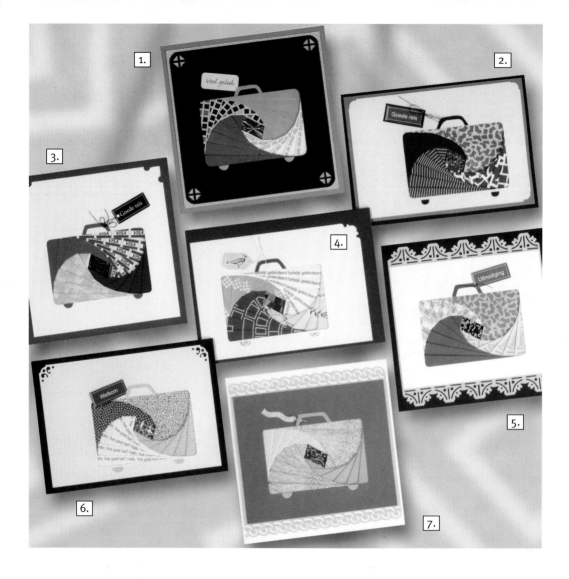

1.
2.
3.
4.
5.
6.
7.

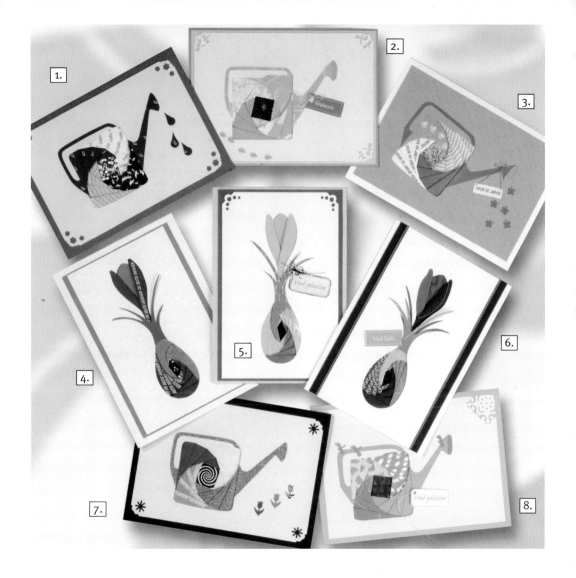

Crocus and watering can

Make sure the crocuses get enough water so that you can enjoy them for a long time.

The crocus is made according to the instructions given for the card on the cover (also see cutting tip 2). The watering can is made according to the instructions given for card 1.

Card on the cover
Card: salmon beige C384 (14.8 x 21 cm) and white (13.6 x 8.9 cm) • Pattern 11 • 2 cm wide strips from 4 different brown blue envelopes • 2 strips from the blue greetings sheet (0.8 x 13.6 cm) • Brown paper (6 x 6 cm) • Gold holographic paper
Cut the crocus out of the back of the white card. Cover the leaf and cut the stem to the same shape as the pattern. Fill the flower before the bulb. Stick the strips from the greetings sheet behind the side.

Card 1
Card: royal blue C495 (14.8 x 21 cm) and lilac C104 (13.7 x 9.5 cm) • Pattern 12 • 2 cm wide strips from 3 different blue envelopes • 2 cm wide strips from the blue greetings sheet • Blue paper (7 x 6 cm) • Silver deco tape • Exchangeable figure punch (Drop) • Multi-corner punch
Punch out the corners of the small card and cut the watering can (only the square) out of the back. Copy the handle and the spout using the light box.

Card 2
Card: mango A575 (14.8 x 21 cm), honey yellow A243 (14.4 x 10.1 cm) and lemon yellow C101 (14 x 9.7 cm) • Pattern 12 • 2 cm wide strips from 4 different orange/green envelopes • Green paper (7 x 6 cm) • Silver deco tape • Text sticker • 3-in-1 corner punch (Bugs)

Card 3
Card: white (14.8 x 21 cm) and pink C352 (13.8 x 9.5 cm) • Pattern 12 • 2 cm wide strips from 3 different grey envelopes • 1.6 cm wide strips from the pink greetings sheet • Grey paper (7 x 6 cm) • Silver deco tape • Mini-punch (Four-leaf clover) • Pencil

Card 4
Card: Firenze embossed beige (14.8 x 21 cm

and 13.5 x 8.2 cm) • Orange paper (13.8 x 9 cm)
• Pattern 11 • 1.5 cm wide strips from 3
different orange envelopes • 1.6 cm wide strips
from the red greetings sheet • Green paper (6 x
6 cm) • Gold deco tape
Fill the flower with a strip from the greetings
sheet and two different orange strips. The
other strips from the greetings sheet are for
sections 2, 6, 10, etc.

Card 5

Card: champagne (14.8 x 21 cm), Havana brown
C502 (14.6 x 9.8 cm) and white (14.2 x 9.1 cm) •
Model 11 • 1.5 cm wide strips from 4 different
yellow/brown envelopes • Green paper (6 x
6cm) • Gold deco tape • Text sticker • Multi-
corner punch
Stick the text sticker on deco tape and cut it
out with a 1 mm border.

Card 6

Card: white (14.8 x 21 cm and 14.8 x 8.2 cm) •
Sheet of purple paper (14.8 x 9.6 cm) and blue
paper (14.8 x 8.5 cm) • Pattern 11 • 1.5 cm wide
strips from 3 different purple envelopes and 4
different brown envelopes • Two pieces of
green paper (6 x 6 cm) • Gold deco tape • Text
sticker

Cut the leaves out of the second piece of green
paper (6 x 6 cm) and stick them on the front of
the card.

Card 7

Card: dark blue A417 (14.8 x 21 cm) and lilac
C104 (13.8 x 9.5 cm) • Pattern 12 • 2 cm wide
strips from 4 different blue/green envelopes •
Blue/green paper (7 x 6 cm) • Silver
holographic paper • Multi-corner punch • Mini-
punch (Tulip)

Card 8

Card: birch green A305 (14.8 x 21 cm) and lime
green C100 (14 x 9.8 cm) • Model 12 • 2 cm
wide strips from 4 different green envelopes •
Green paper (7 x 6 cm) • Silver holographic
paper • Text sticker • Mosaic punch (Art) • 3-in-
1 corner punch (Bugs)

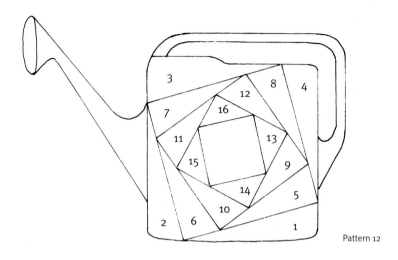

Pattern 12

Thanks to:
Kars & Co BV in Ochten, the Netherlands.
Koninklijke Talens in Apeldoorn, the Netherlands for supplying the card
Romak in Hillegom, the Netherlands for the oval cards
Nederlandse Vereniging voor Papierknipkunst for the cutting tips. Info: +31-224 – 541582

The materials used can be ordered by shopkeepers from:
Avec B.V. in Waalwijk, the Netherlands
Kars & Co BV in Ochten, the Netherlands.